THE U[illegible] FRENCH BULLDOG JOKE BOOK

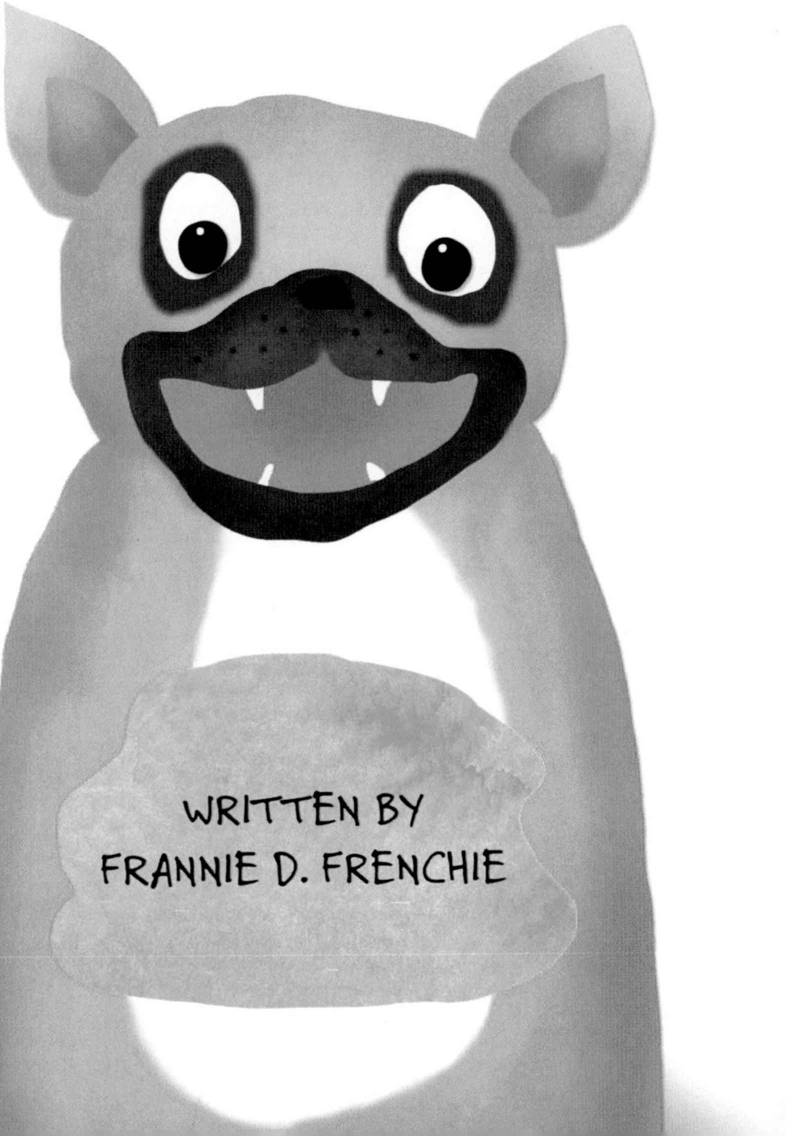

WRITTEN BY
FRANNIE D. FRENCHIE

THE ULTIMATE
FRENCH BULLDOG
JOKE BOOK

PUGCITY PRESS
WWW.PUGJOKES.COM

ISBN-13: 978-1979655798
ISBN-10: 1979655790

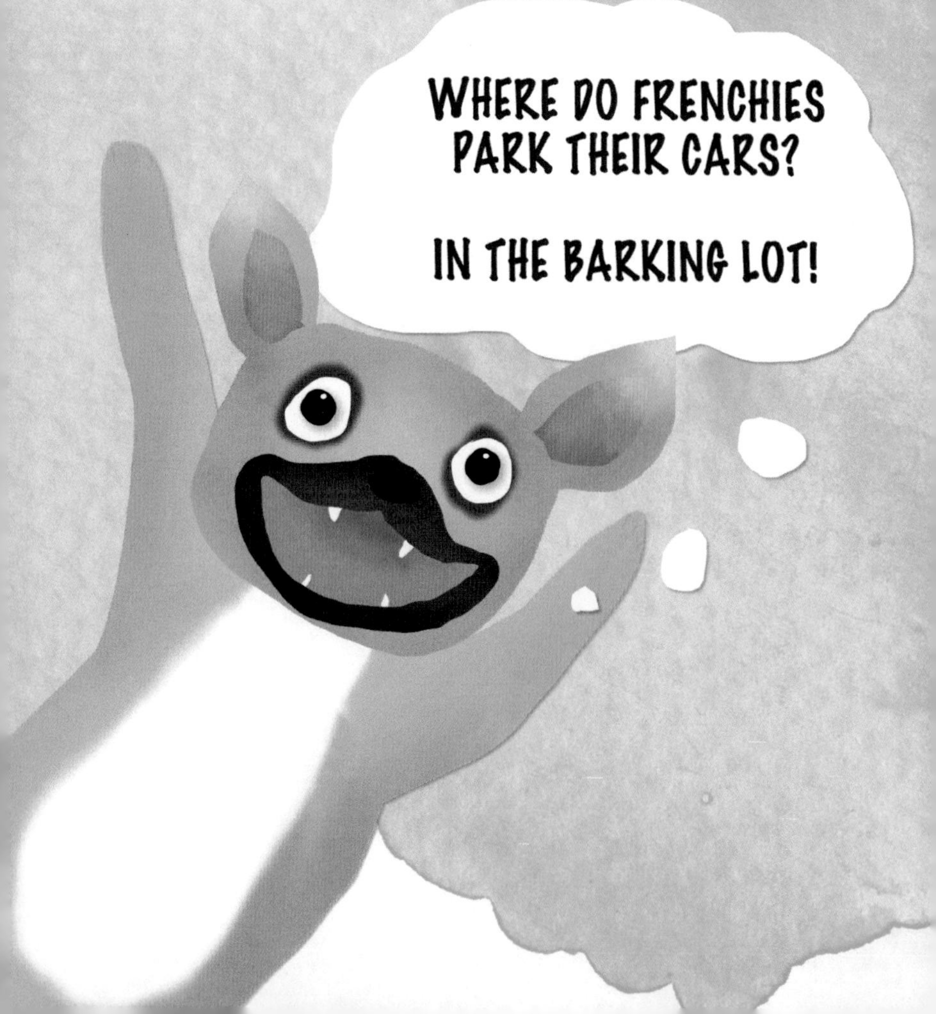
WHERE DO FRENCHIES PARK THEIR CARS?
IN THE BARKING LOT!

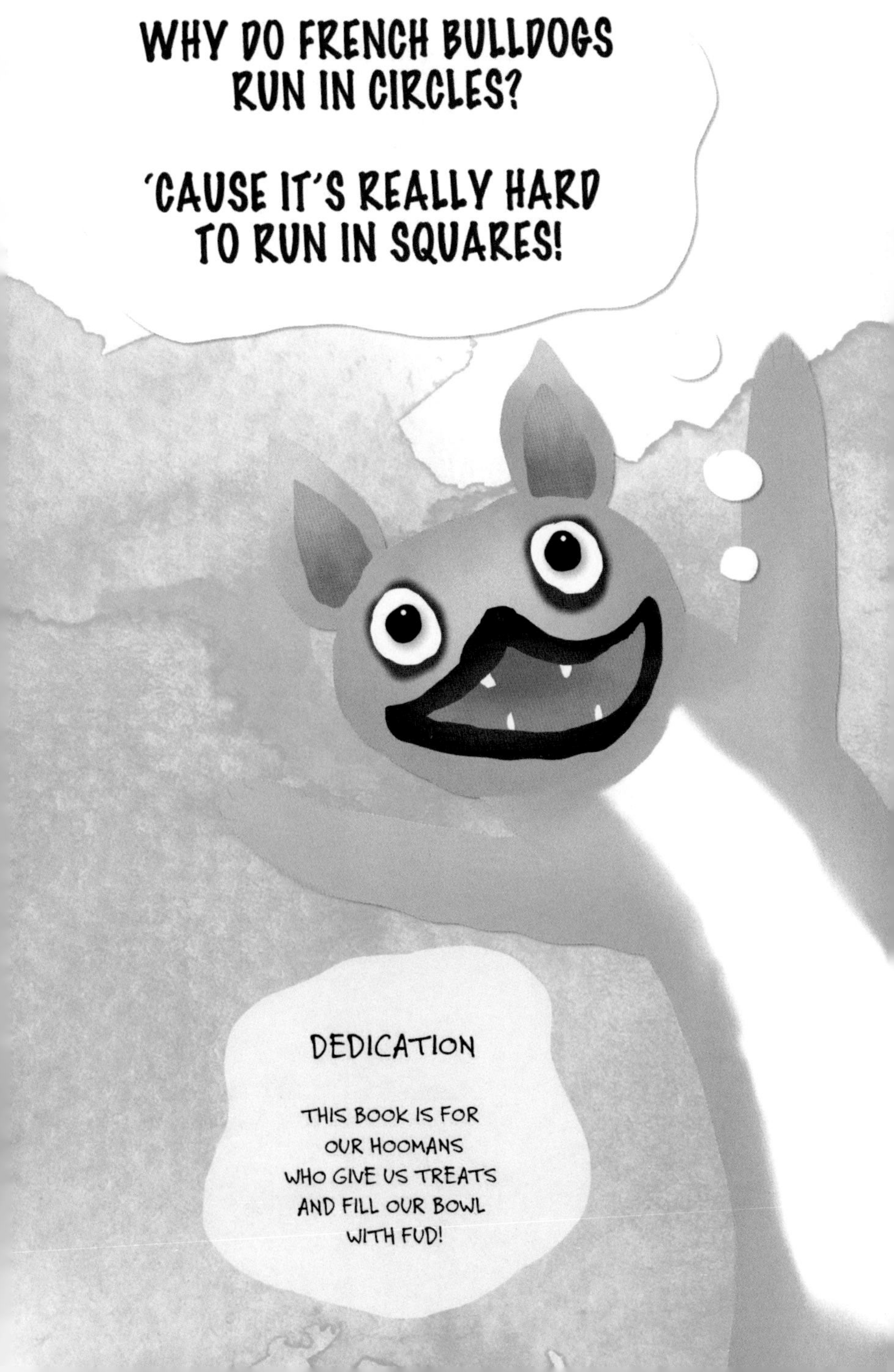
WHY DO FRENCH BULLDOGS RUN IN CIRCLES?
'CAUSE IT'S REALLY HARD TO RUN IN SQUARES!
DEDICATION
THIS BOOK IS FOR OUR HOOMANS WHO GIVE US TREATS AND FILL OUR BOWL WITH FUD!

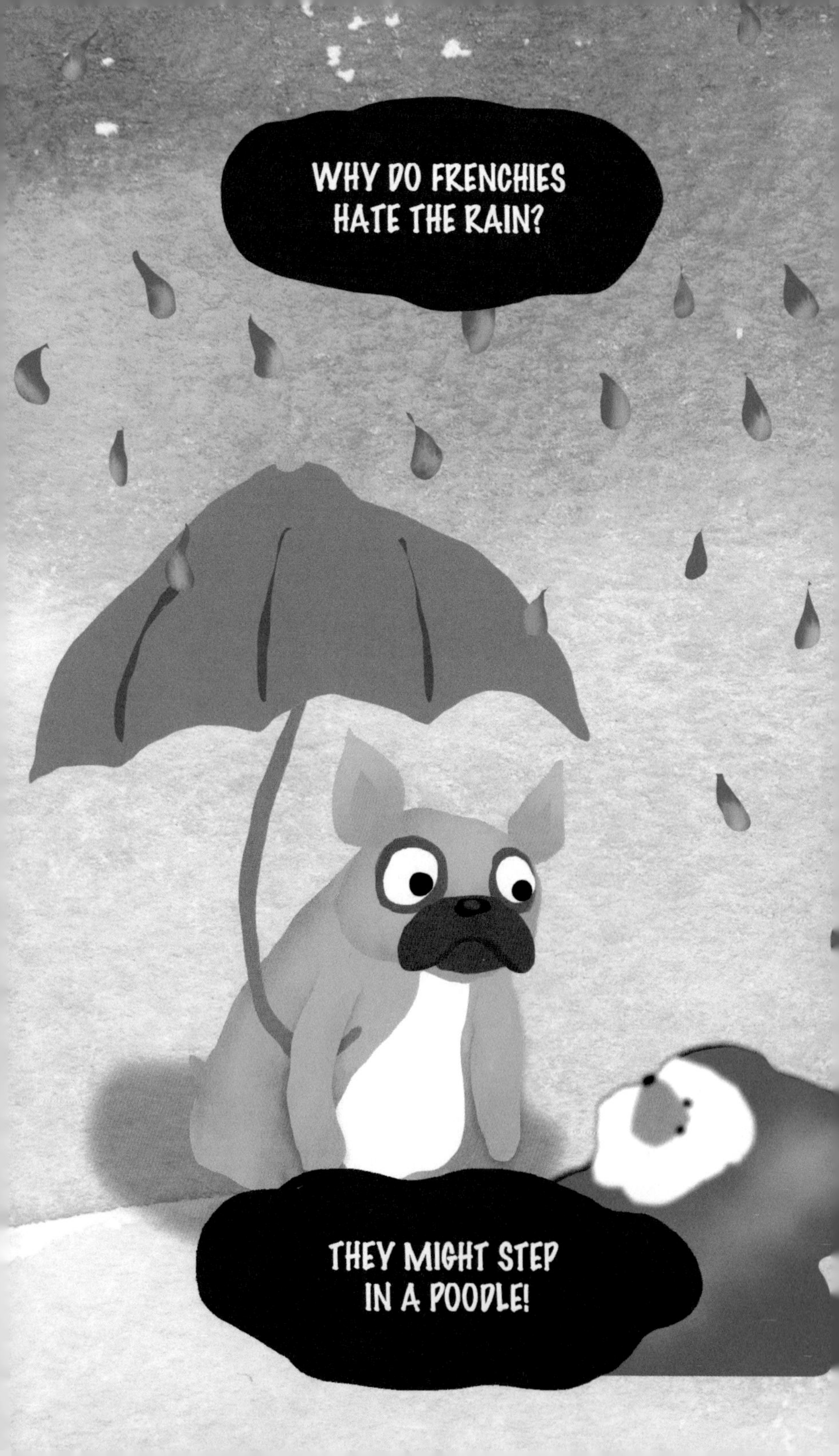
WHY DO FRENCHIES HATE THE RAIN?
THEY MIGHT STEP IN A POODLE!

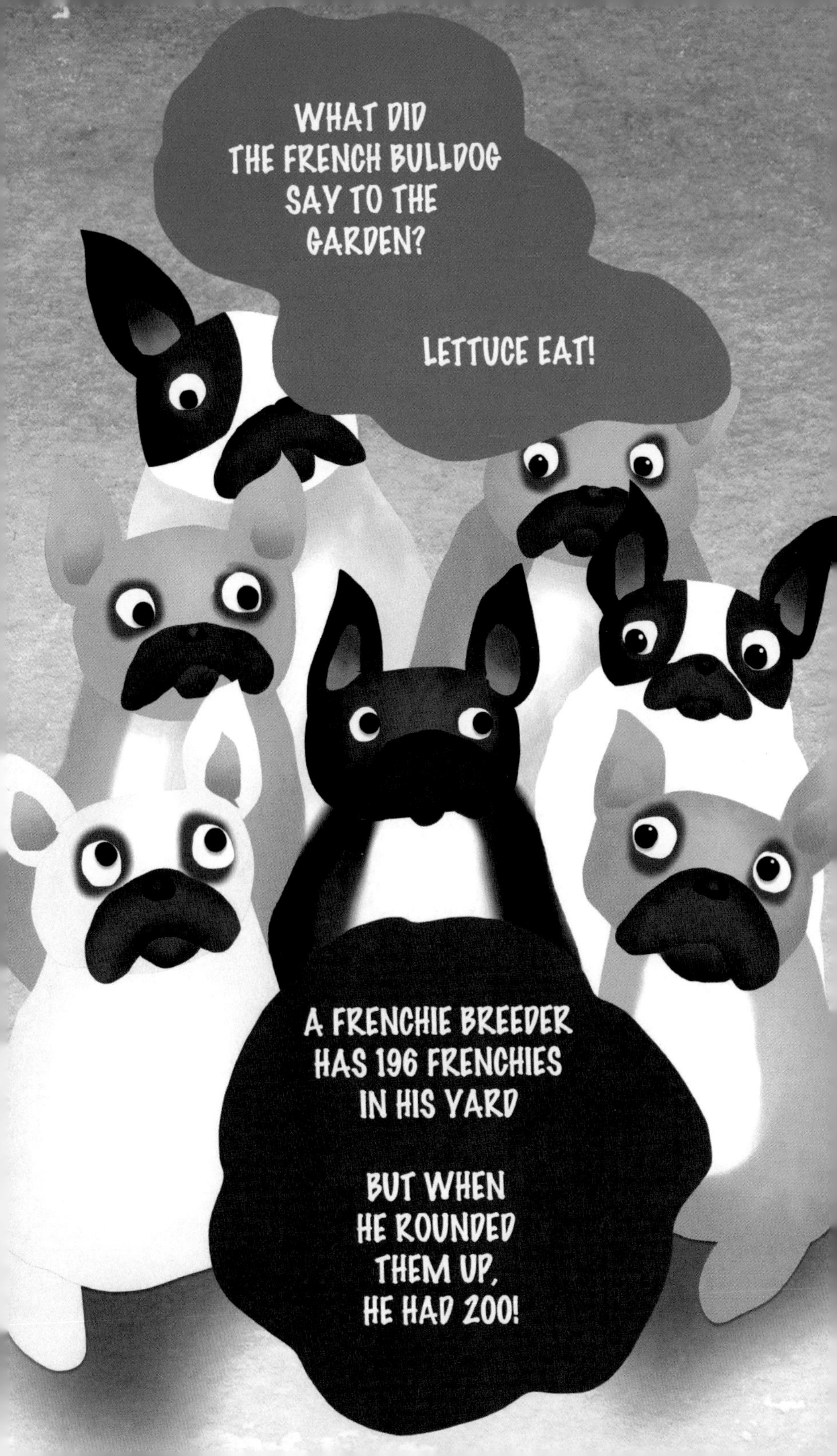
WHAT DID THE FRENCH BULLDOG SAY TO THE GARDEN?
LETTUCE EAT!
A FRENCHIE BREEDER HAS 196 FRENCHIES IN HIS YARD
BUT WHEN HE ROUNDED THEM UP, HE HAD 200!

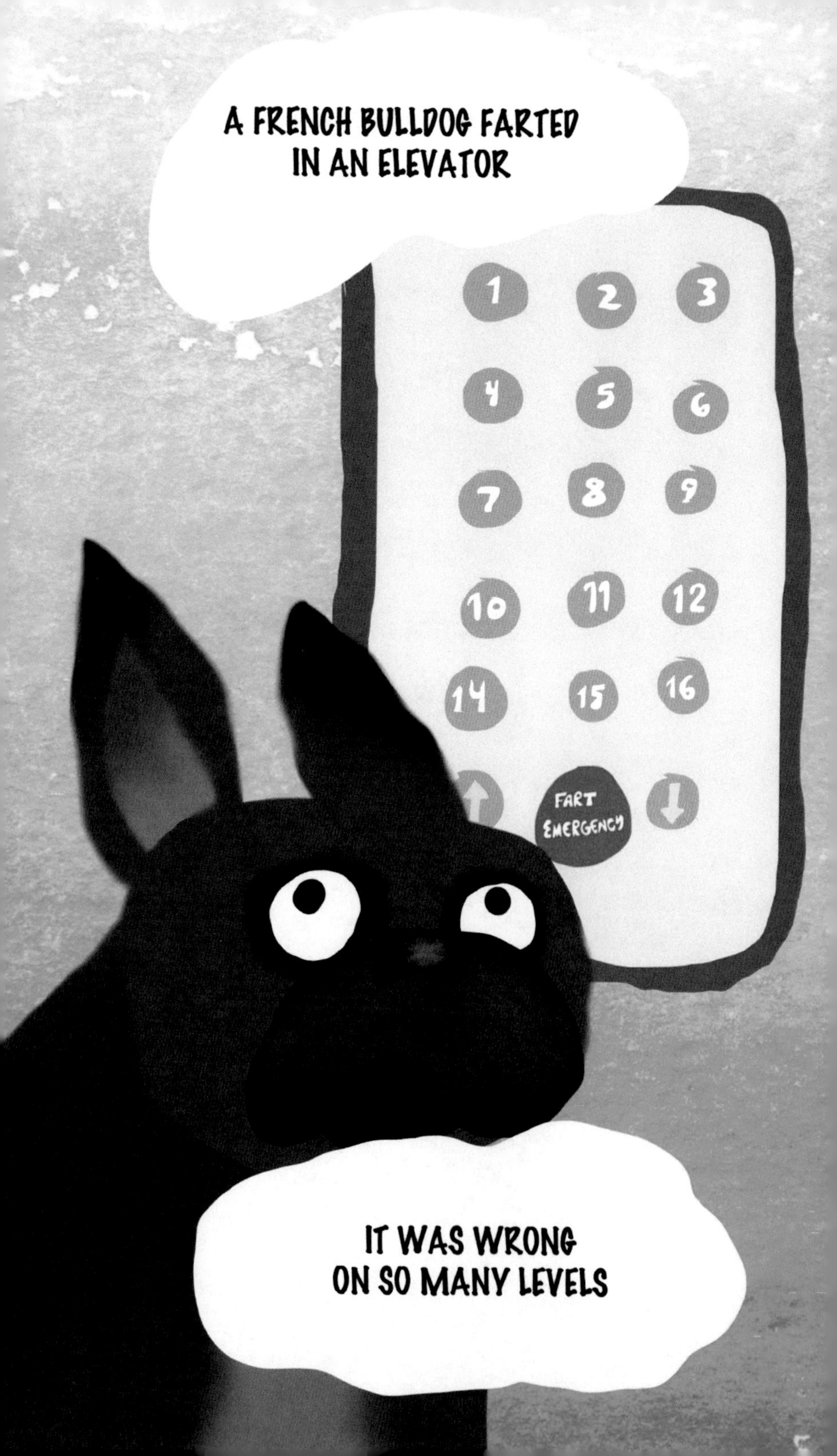
A FRENCH BULLDOG FARTED IN AN ELEVATOR
1 2 3 4 5 6 7 8 9 10 11 12 14 15 16
FART EMERGENCY
IT WAS WRONG ON SO MANY LEVELS

TWO OLD FRENCHIES
ARE IN THE LIBRARY.
ONE LEANS OVER
AND WHISPERS

"I JUST LET OUT
A LONG, SILENT FART!
WHAT SHOULD I DO?"

THE OTHER REPLIES,
"FIRST OFF, REPLACE THE
BATTERIES IN YOUR
HEARING AID"

WHY DO FRENCH BULLDOG
FARTS SMELL?

FOR THE BENEFIT OF PEOPLE
WHO ARE
HEARING IMPAIRED!

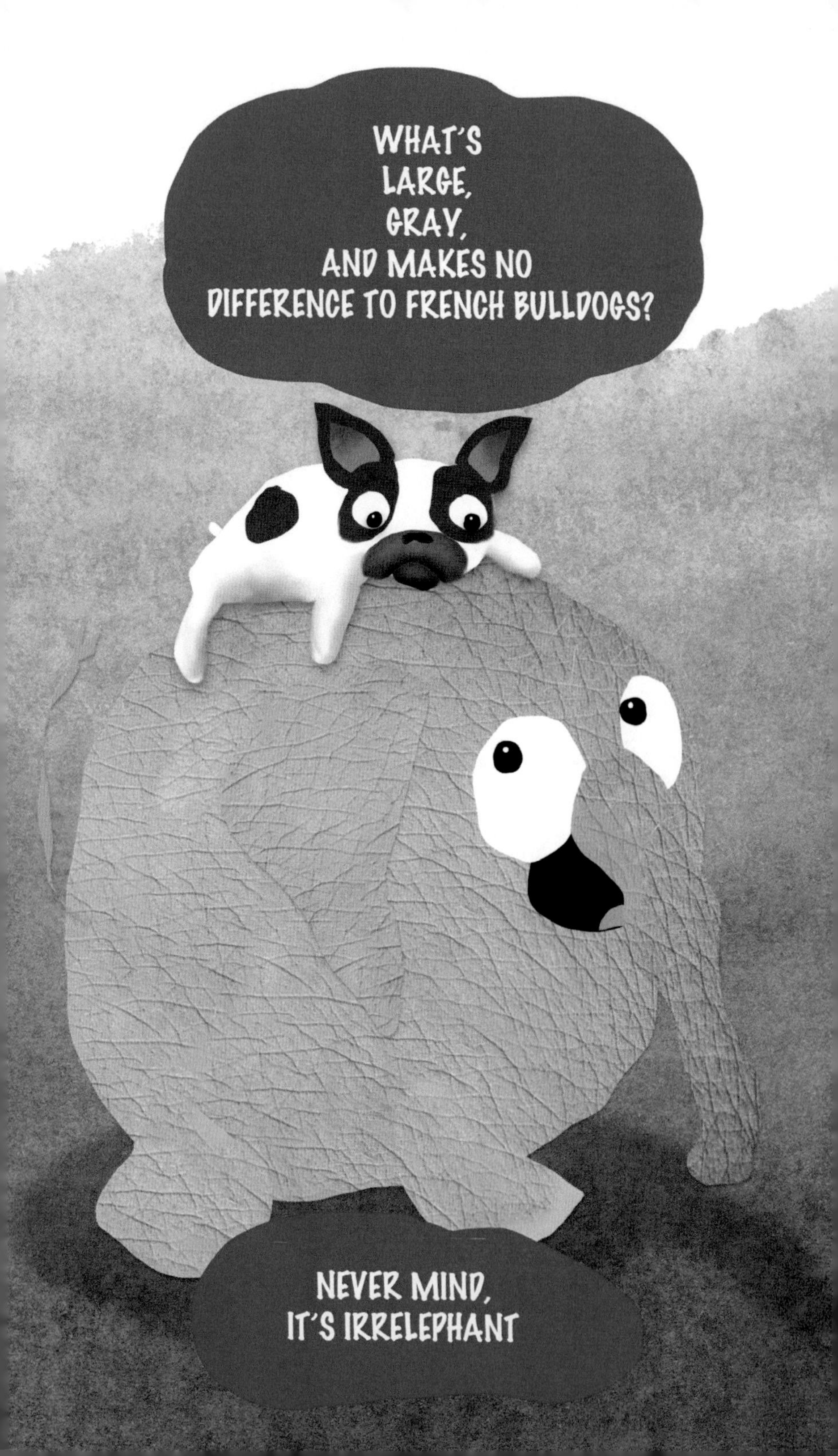
WHAT'S LARGE, GRAY, AND MAKES NO DIFFERENCE TO FRENCH BULLDOGS?
NEVER MIND, IT'S IRRELEPHANT

A FRENCHIE, A KING CHARLES,
AND A POMERANIAN
WERE ALL LOST IN THE
DESERT WHEN THEY
FOUND A MAGIC LAMP!
A GENIE POPPED OUT AND
GRANTED THEM EACH ONE WISH.

THE POMERANIAN WISHED
SHE WAS BACK HOME.
POOF!
SHE WAS BACK HOME.

THE KING CHARLES WISHED
SHE WAS WITH HER FAMILY.
POOF,
SHE WAS BACK HOME
WITH HER FAMILY.

THE FRENCHIE SAID,
"AWWWWW, I WISH MY
FRIENDS WERE HERE"

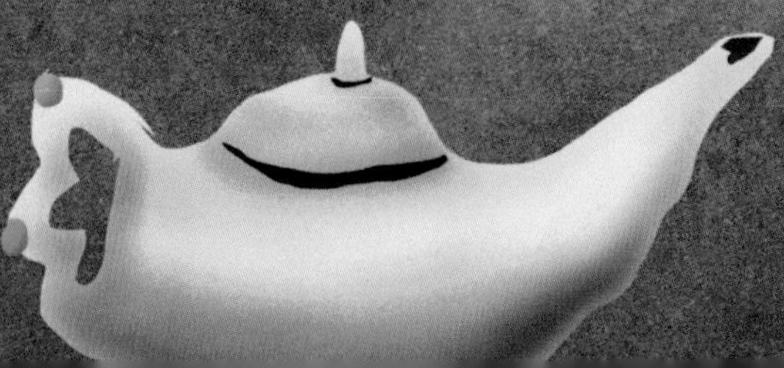

WHY DO
FRENCHIE VAMPIRES
BELIEVE EVERYTHING
YOU TELL THEM?

BECAUSE
THEY'RE SUCKERS

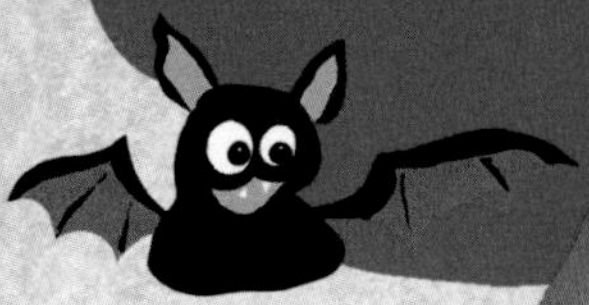

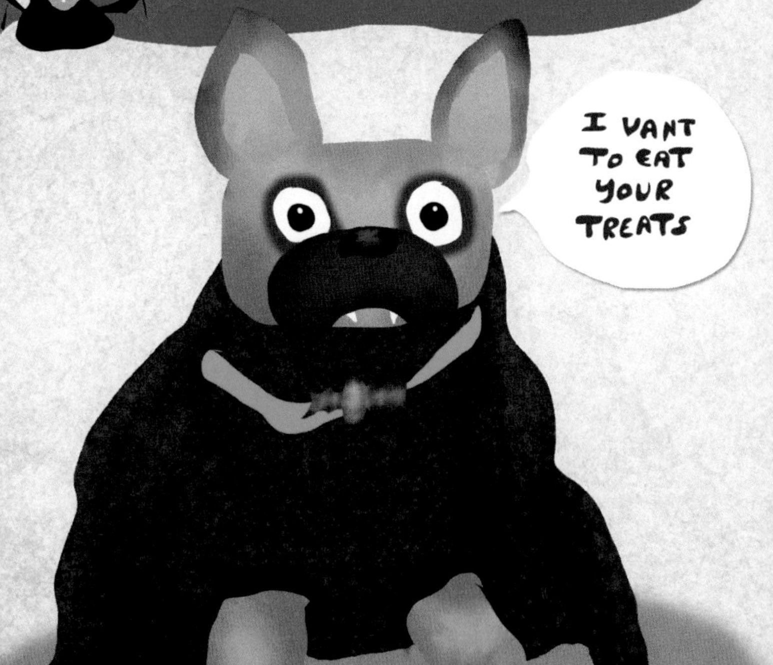

WHAT DO YOU GET WHEN
YOU TRY TO CROSS A FRENCH BULLDOG
WITH A COMPUTER?

A LOT OF LITTLE BYTES.

WHAT'S A FRENCHIES
FAVORITE PIZZA?

PUPPERONI

WHAT KIND OF FRENCH BULLDOGS
DONT LIKE PIZZA?

WEIR-DOUGHS!

WHAT'S THE
DIFFERENCE
BETWEEN A PIZZA
AND THESE
PIZZA FRENCHIE JOKES?

THESE FRENCHIE JOKES
CAN'T BE TOPPED!

OK, OK, ONE MORE
FRENCH BULLDOG PIZZA JOKE?

NAH, NEVER MIND,
IT'S TOO CHEESY!

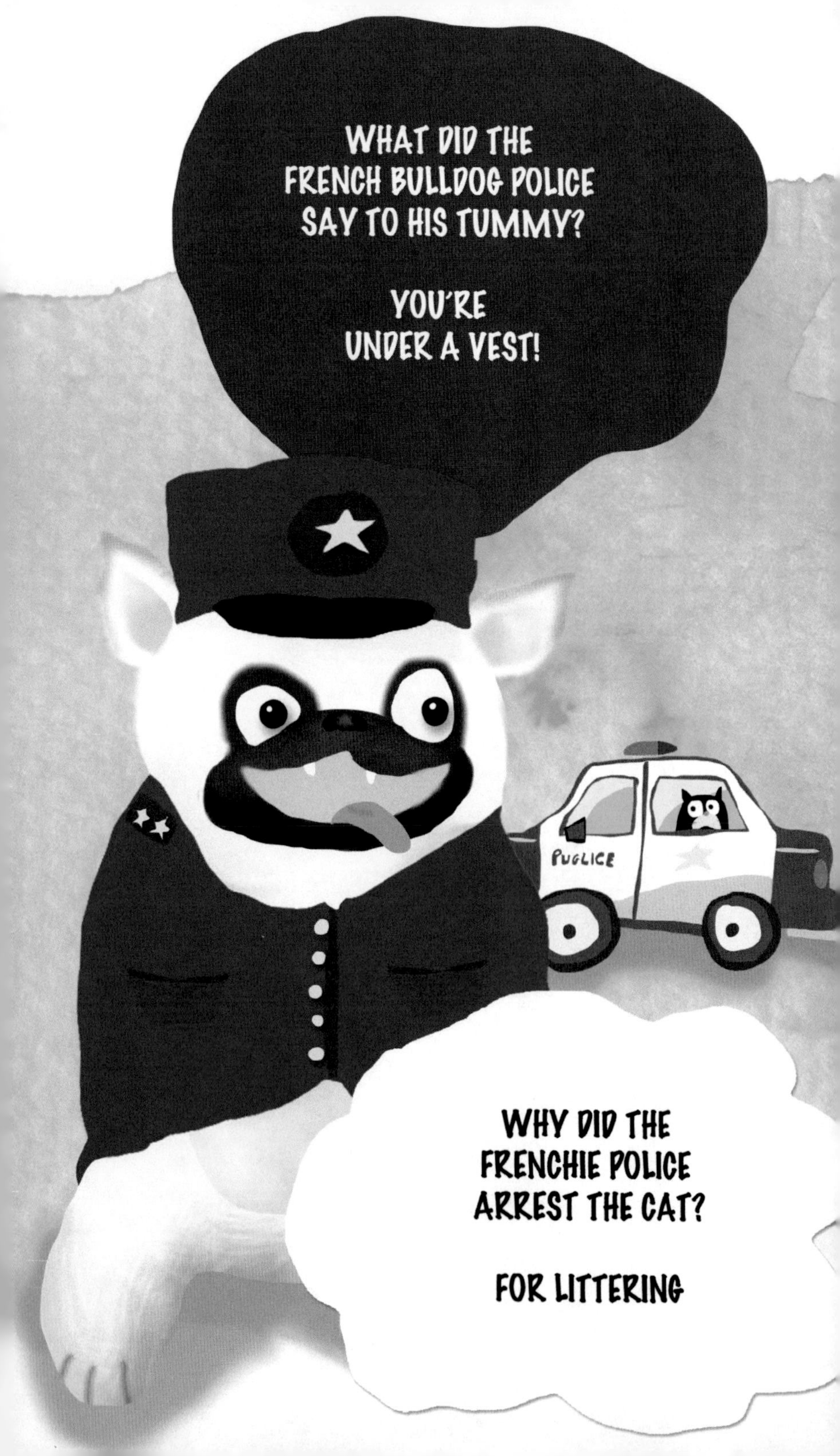
WHAT DID THE FRENCH BULLDOG POLICE SAY TO HIS TUMMY?
YOU'RE UNDER A VEST!
PUGLICE
WHY DID THE FRENCHIE POLICE ARREST THE CAT?
FOR LITTERING

WHY DON'T
FRENCH BULLDOGS WRITE WITH
DULL PENCILS?

BECAUSE
IT'S POINTLESS

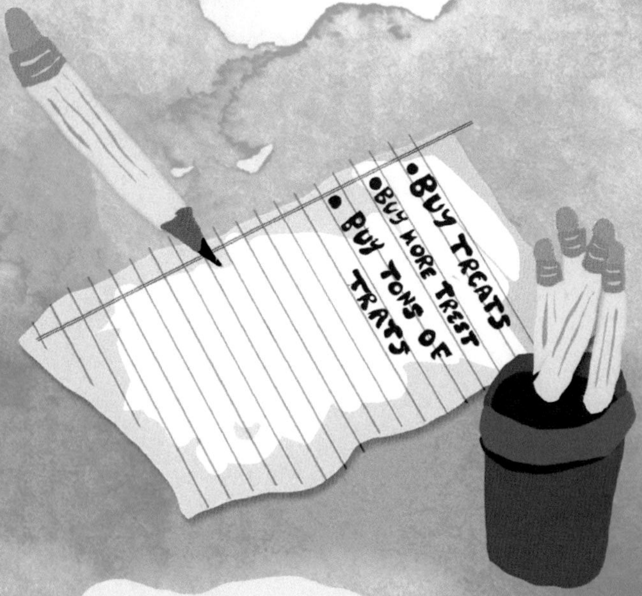
•BUY TREATS
•BUY MORE TREST
• BUY TONS OF TRATS

HOW DID
THE FRENCH BULLDOG
FEEL AFTER
SEEING THE
NEW SCOTTISH
DOG MOVIE?

TERRIER-FIED!

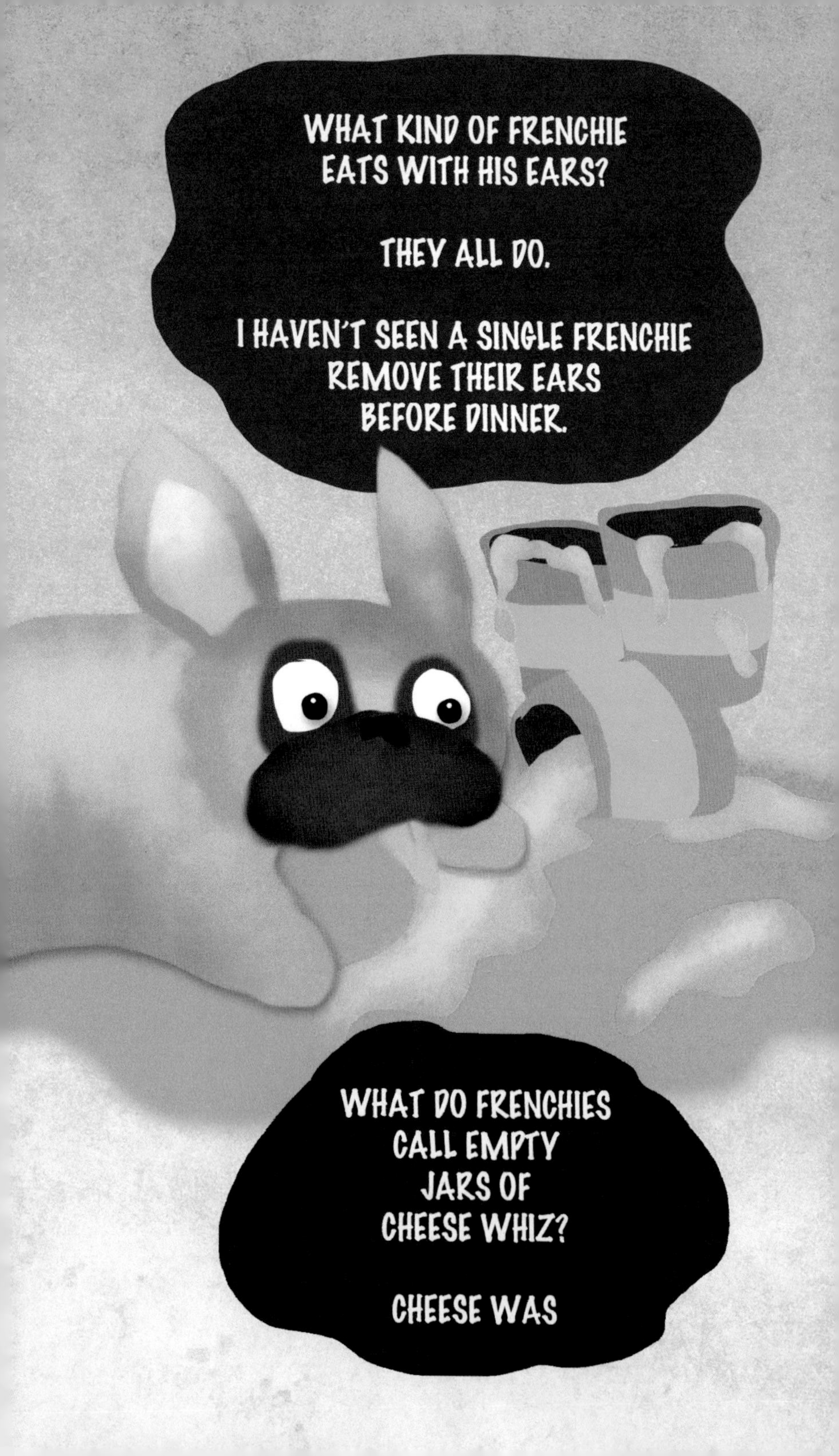
WHAT KIND OF FRENCHIE EATS WITH HIS EARS?
THEY ALL DO.
I HAVEN'T SEEN A SINGLE FRENCHIE REMOVE THEIR EARS BEFORE DINNER.
WHAT DO FRENCHIES CALL EMPTY JARS OF CHEESE WHIZ?
CHEESE WAS

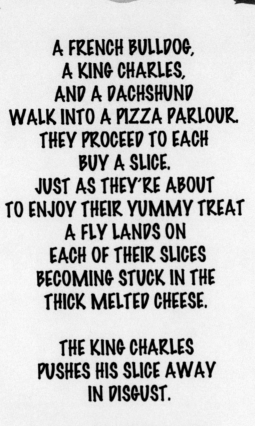

A FRENCH BULLDOG,
A KING CHARLES,
AND A DACHSHUND
WALK INTO A PIZZA PARLOUR.
THEY PROCEED TO EACH
BUY A SLICE.
JUST AS THEY'RE ABOUT
TO ENJOY THEIR YUMMY TREAT
A FLY LANDS ON
EACH OF THEIR SLICES
BECOMING STUCK IN THE
THICK MELTED CHEESE.

THE KING CHARLES
PUSHES HIS SLICE AWAY
IN DISGUST.

THE DACHSHUND FISHES
THE FLY OUT OF THE CHEESE
AND EATS IT,
SCHLURP!

THE FRENCHIE ALSO PICKS THE FLY
OUT OF HIS SLICE,
HOLDS IT OVER THE PLATE
AND STARTS YELLING
"SPIT IT OUT! SPIT IT OUT!"

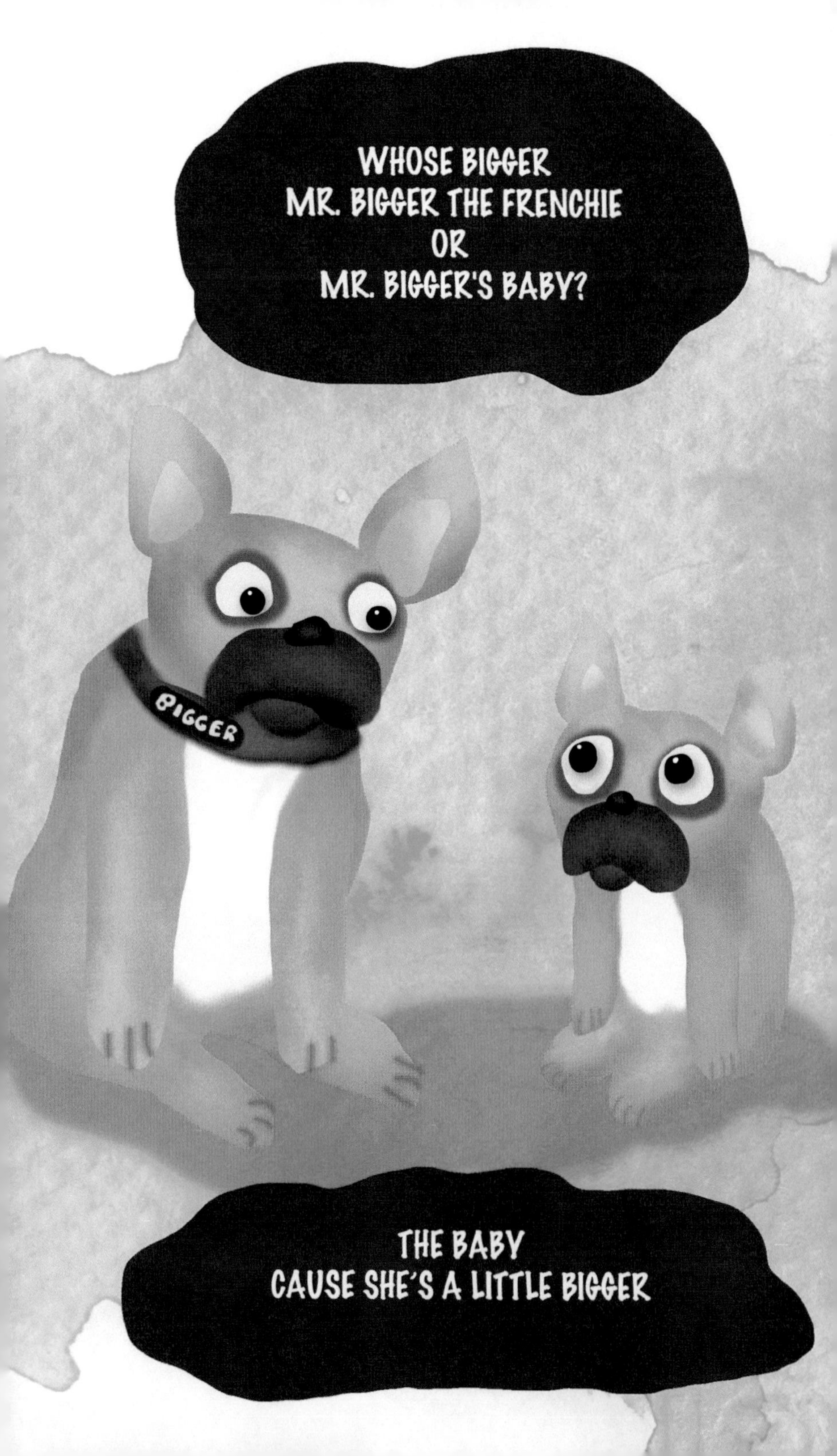
WHOSE BIGGER
MR. BIGGER THE FRENCHIE
OR
MR. BIGGER'S BABY?
BIGGER
THE BABY
CAUSE SHE'S A LITTLE BIGGER

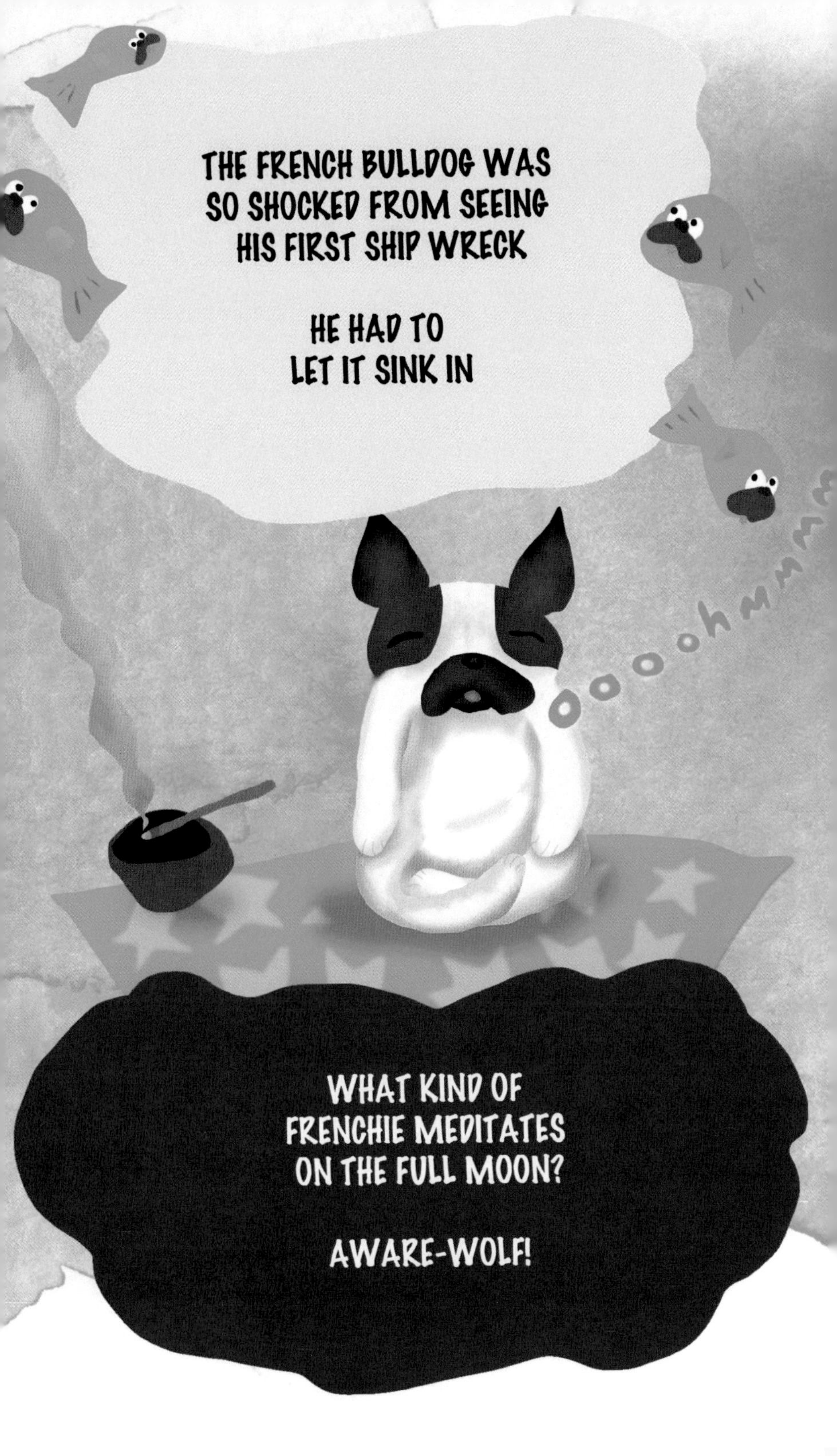
THE FRENCH BULLDOG WAS SO SHOCKED FROM SEEING HIS FIRST SHIP WRECK
HE HAD TO LET IT SINK IN
WHAT KIND OF FRENCHIE MEDITATES ON THE FULL MOON?
AWARE-WOLF!

WHAT HAPPENS
WHEN A FRENCH BULLDOG
RUNS OVER A FROG?

HE GETS TOAD!

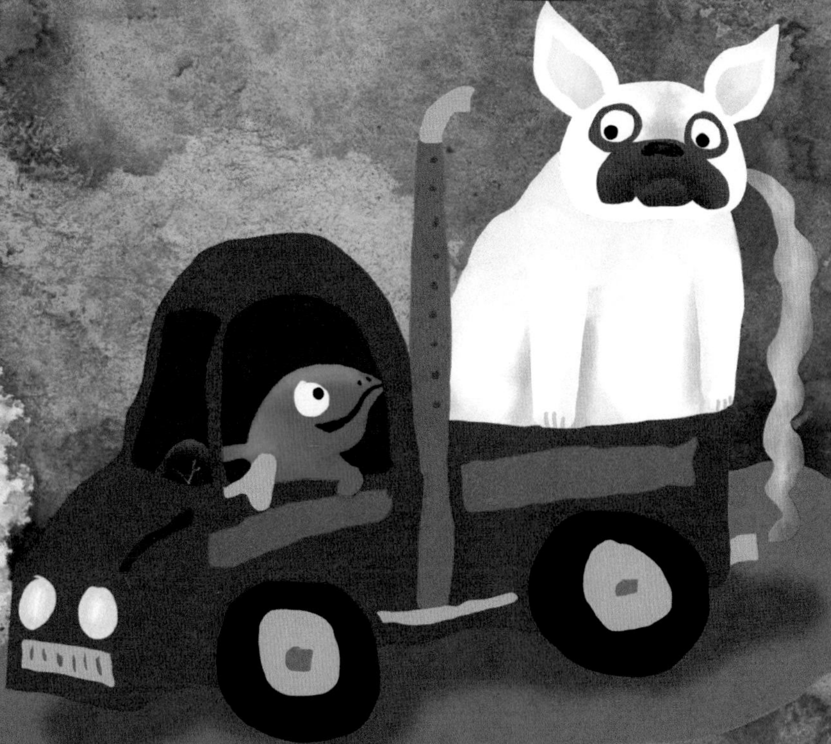

HOW DO YOU GET A FRENCHIE TO STOP BARKING
IN THE BACK SEAT WHEN YOUR DRIVING?

LET HIM BARK IN THE FRONT SEAT!

A FRENCH BULLDOG OWNER
COMES HOME FROM
THE INTERNATIONAL MARKET

"HERE BOY!
YOU WANT
SOME BRAZILIAN TREATS?"

THE FRENCHIE REPLIES

"OH MY GOSH!
I'M SO LUCKY!!!
WAIT...
HOW MANY IS A
BRAZILIAN?"

I TOOK MY FRENCH BULLDOG
TO THE VET.

SHE SAID
"YOUR FRENCHIE IS OVERWEIGHT"

I TOLD HER
"I WANT A SECOND OPINION!"

SHE REPLIED
"HE'S ALSO PRETTY CUTE!"

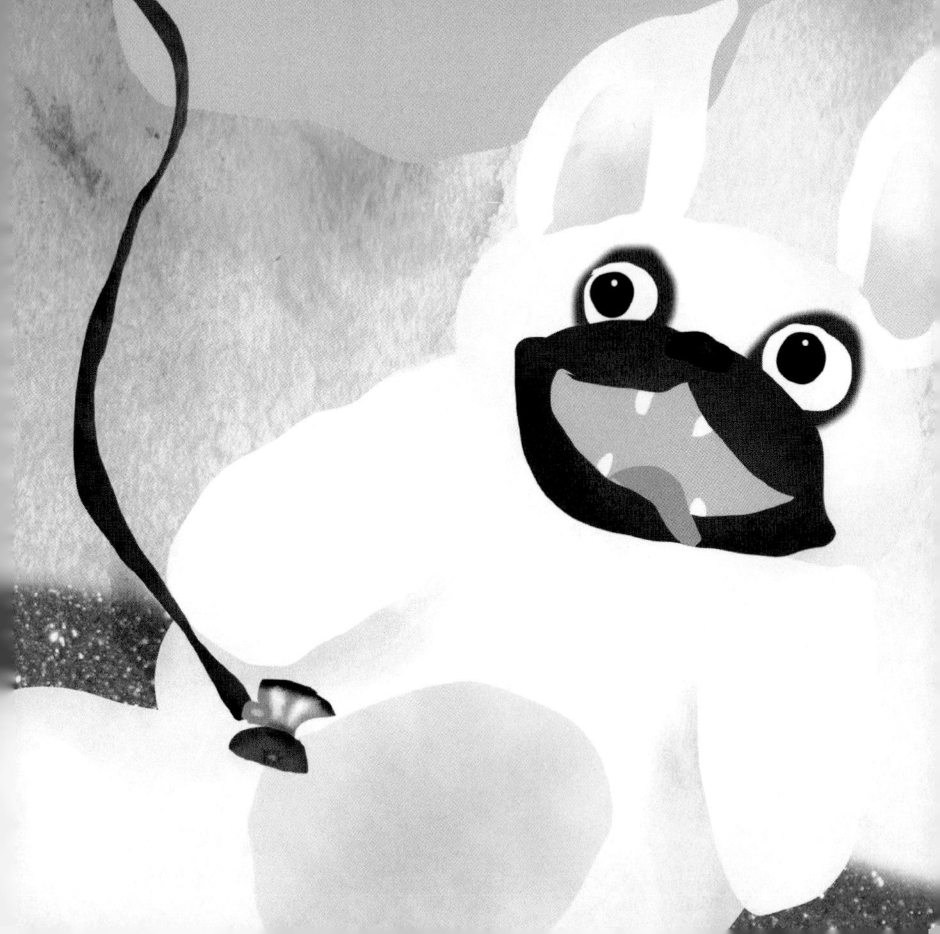

THE FRENCH BULLDOG WAS
FEELING
LOW SELF ESTEEM

"I LOOK FAT"
SHE SAID TO
THE KING CHARLES
"CAN YOU GIVE ME
A COMPLIMENT?"

THE KING CHARLES REPLIED
"YOU'VE GOT PERFECT EYESIGHT"

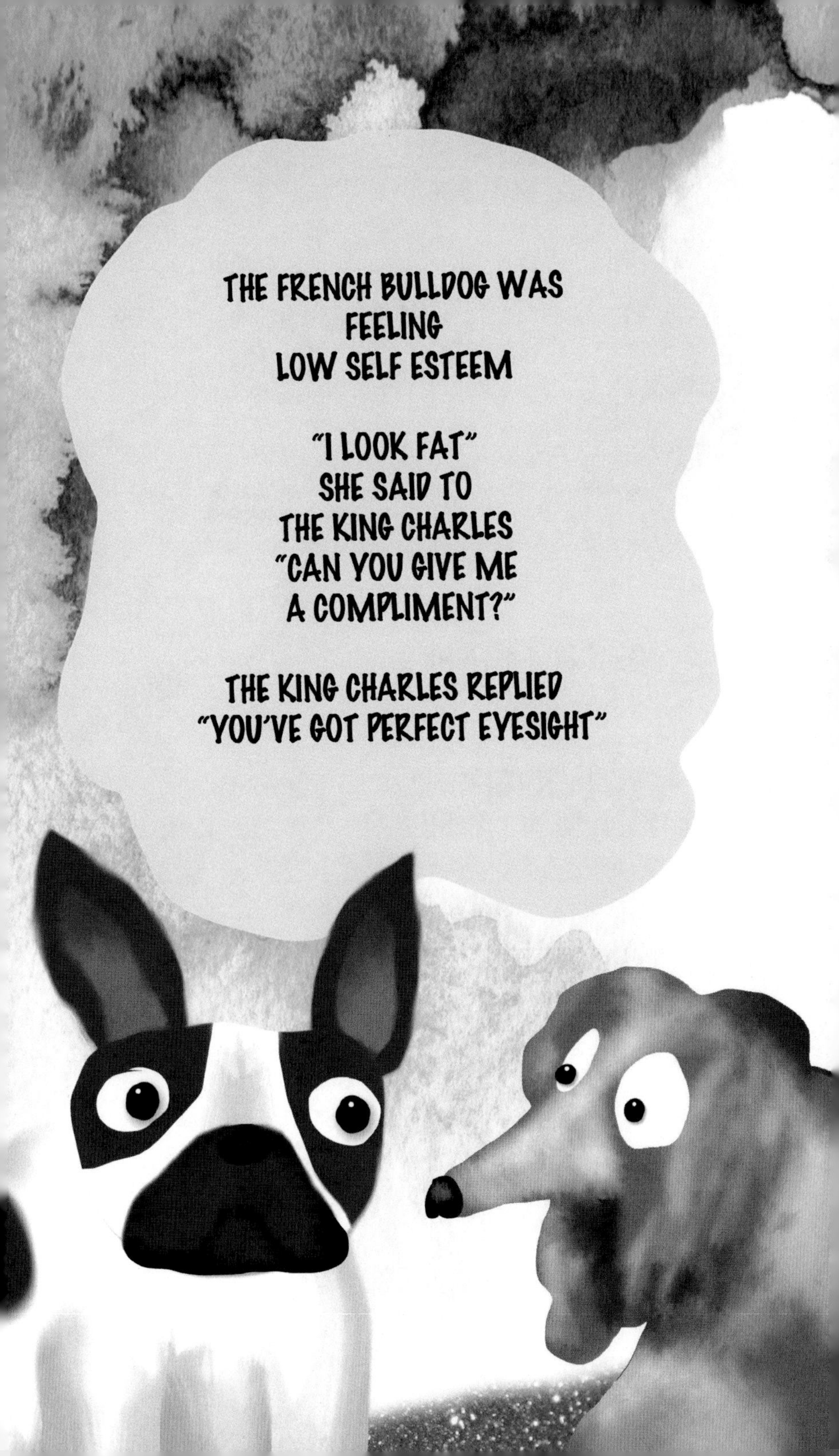

WHY DID THE
VEGETARIAN
FRENCH BULLDOG BLUSH?

HE SAW THE
SALAD DRESSING

WHEN DO FRENCHIES
SAY "MOO"?

WHEN THEY
LEARN A NEW LANGUAGE!

WHAT DID THE FRENCHIE SAY
WAS ON TOP OF THE HOUSE?

DA ROOF
ROOF ROOF!

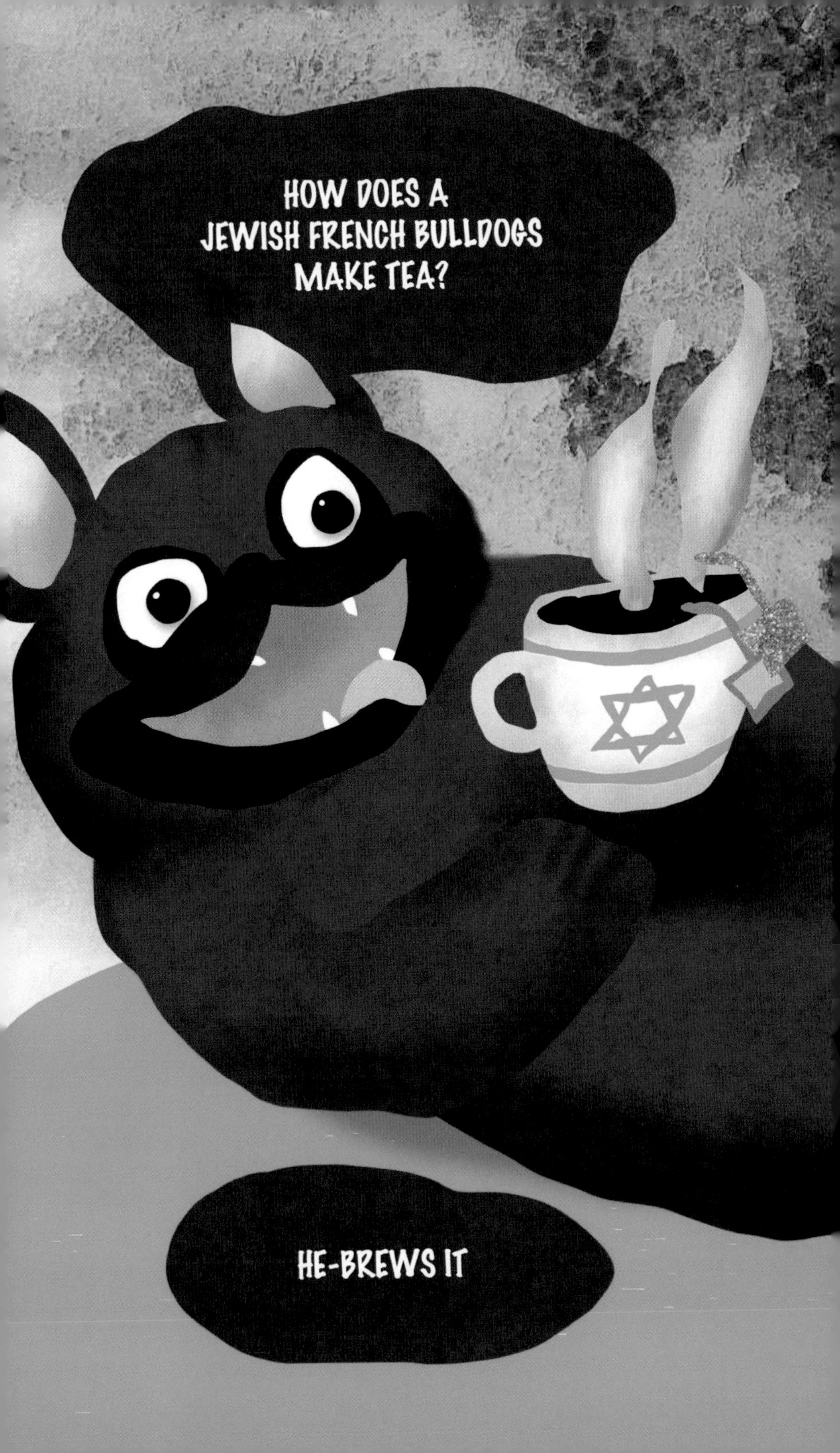
HOW DOES A JEWISH FRENCH BULLDOGS MAKE TEA?
HE-BREWS IT

WHAT'S A FRENCH BULLDOGS
FAVORITE
MUSICAL
INSTRUMENT?

THE DINNER BELL

WHATS A FRENCHIES
SECOND FAVORITE
INSTRUMENT?

A TROM BONE!

BUT DID YOU
HEAR ABOUT
THE FRENCHIE WHO
PLAYED PIANO?

HIS BACH
WAS WORSE
THAN HIS BITE!

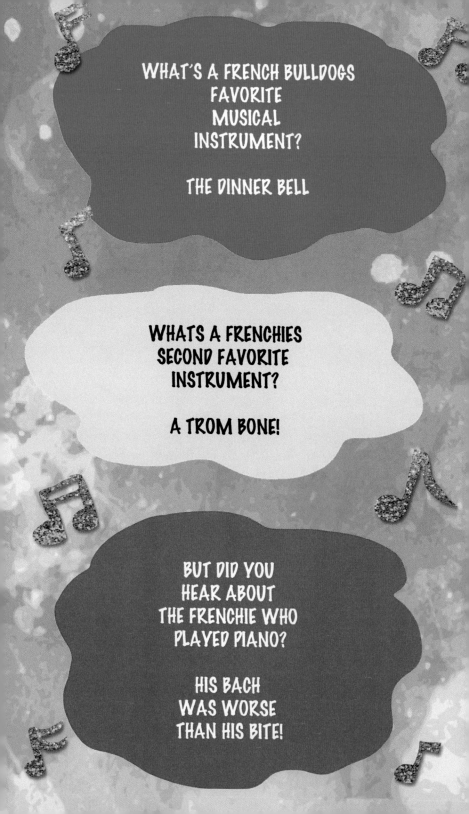

MY FRENCHIE IS
IN SHAPE

UNFORTUNATELY
IT'S THE
WRONG ONE

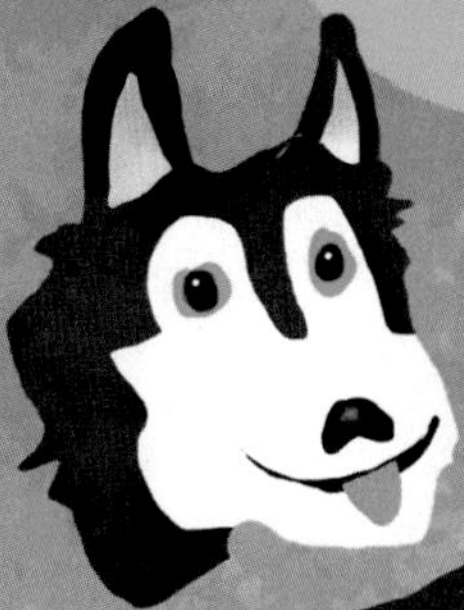

MY FRENCHIE
WAS SO FAT

HE TURNED
INTO A HUSKY!

A MAN TAKES HIS FRENCHIE
TO THE VET AND SAYS
"MY DOG'S CROSS-EYED!
IS THERE ANYTHING YOU CAN DO FOR HIM?"

"WELL" SAYS THE VET.
"LET'S HAVE A LOOK AT HIM."
SO HE PICKS UP THE LAB
AND EXAMINES HIS EYES,
THEN CHECKS HIS TEETH,
FINALLY, HE GIVES A BIG SIGH
AND SAYS "IM GOING
TO HAVE TO PUT HIM DOWN."

"WHAT!?! BECAUSE HE'S CROSS-EYED?"

"NO, BECAUSE HE'S REALLY HEAVY!"

WHAT DID THE
FRENCH BULLDOG SAY
AFTER EATING
AT THE DALMATIAN
RESTAURANT?

THAT REALLY HIT THE SPOT!

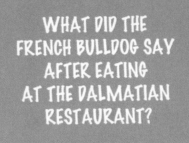

THAT FRENCHIE
IS A REALLY
MEAN COOK!

HE WHIPS
THE CREAM
AND
BEATS THE EGGS

HOW CAN YOU
TELL IF A FRENCHIE
IS A GOOD COOK?

HE MAKES GREAT
USE OF HIS THYME!

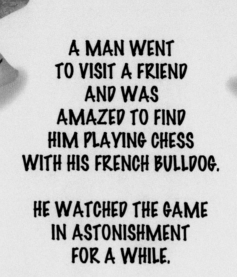

A MAN WENT
TO VISIT A FRIEND
AND WAS
AMAZED TO FIND
HIM PLAYING CHESS
WITH HIS FRENCH BULLDOG.

HE WATCHED THE GAME
IN ASTONISHMENT
FOR A WHILE.

"I CAN HARDLY BELIEVE MY EYES!"
HE EXCLAIMED.
"THAT FRENCHIE IS
THE SMARTEST DOG
I'VE EVER SEEN."

"NAH,
HE'S NOT
SO SMART,"
THE FRIEND REPLIED.

"I'VE BEATEN HIM
THREE GAMES
OUT OF FIVE."

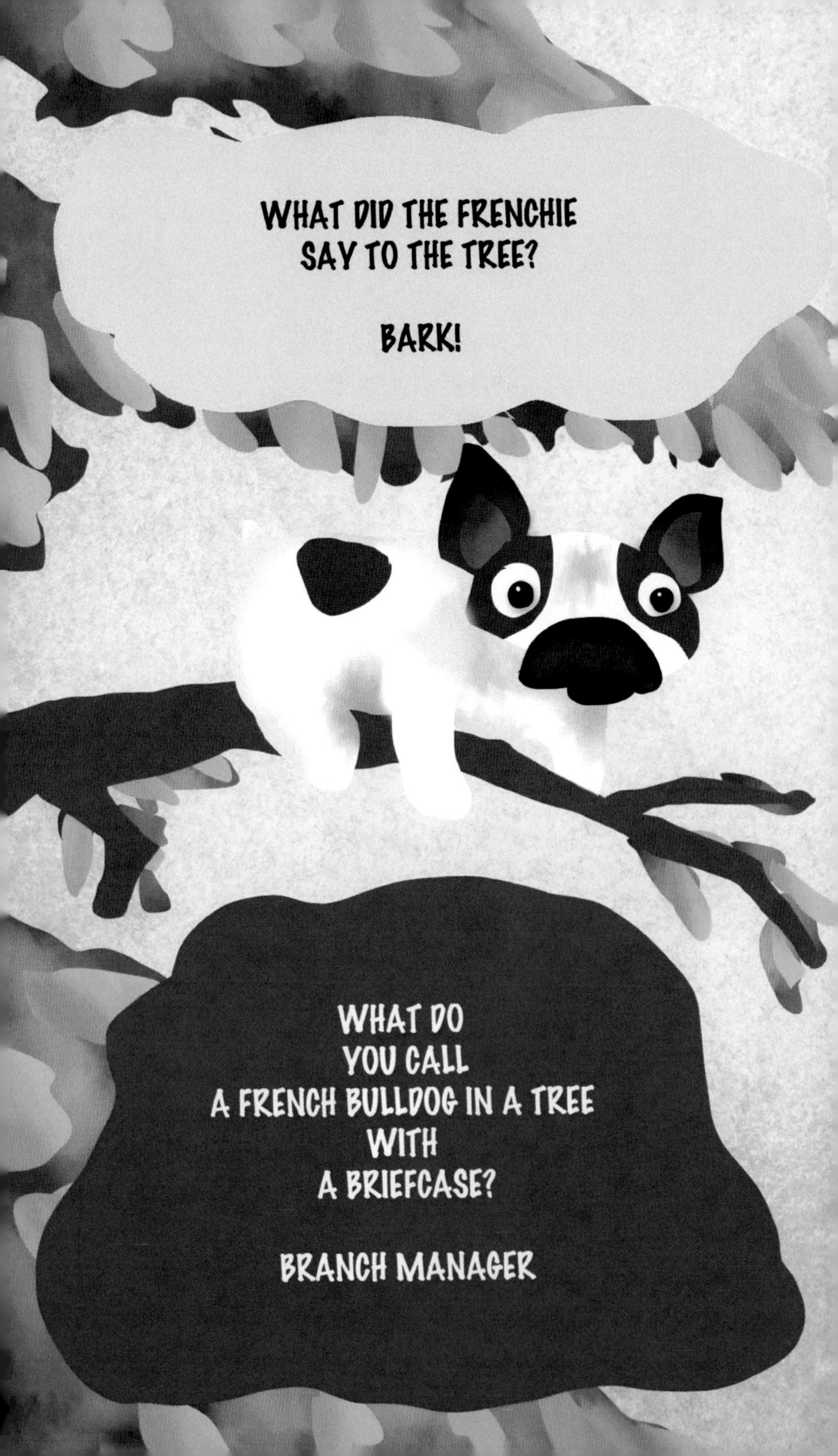
WHAT DID THE FRENCHIE SAY TO THE TREE?
BARK!
WHAT DO YOU CALL A FRENCH BULLDOG IN A TREE WITH A BRIEFCASE?
BRANCH MANAGER

WHILE AT A
DOGGY DINNER PARTY
A FRENCHIE FARTS.

THE
KING CHARLES SAYS
"HOW DARE YOU
FART IN FRONT OF ME!"

THE FRENCHIE REPLIES
"I'M SORRY,
I DIDN'T REALIZE
IT WAS YOUR TURN"

MY FRENCH BULLDOG IS DEPRESSED

HOW DO YOU KNOW?

EVERY TIME
I ASK HOW HIS LIFE'S GOING,
ALL HE SAYS IS
"RUFF!"

SOMEONE STOLE
MY FRENCH BULLDOG
MOOD RING!

I HAVE NO IDEA
HOW I FEEL
ABOUT IT!

KNOCK KNOCK
WHOSE THERE

DOORBELL
REPAIR FRENCHIE!

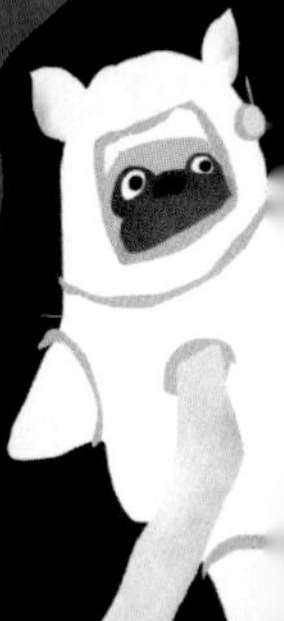

HOW DO FRENCH BULLDOG
ASTRONAUGHTS
ORGANIZE
SPACE PARTIES?

THEY PLANET!

DID YOU SEE THOSE
FRENCH BULLDOGS
JUMPING ON TRAMPOLINES?

IT MUST BE SPRING!

WHATS MORE
AMAZING THAN
A TALKING FRENCHIE?

A SPELLING BEE!

WHY DO
FRENCH BULLDOGS ALWAYS
WORK AS BAKERS?

FOR THE
EXTRA DOUGH!

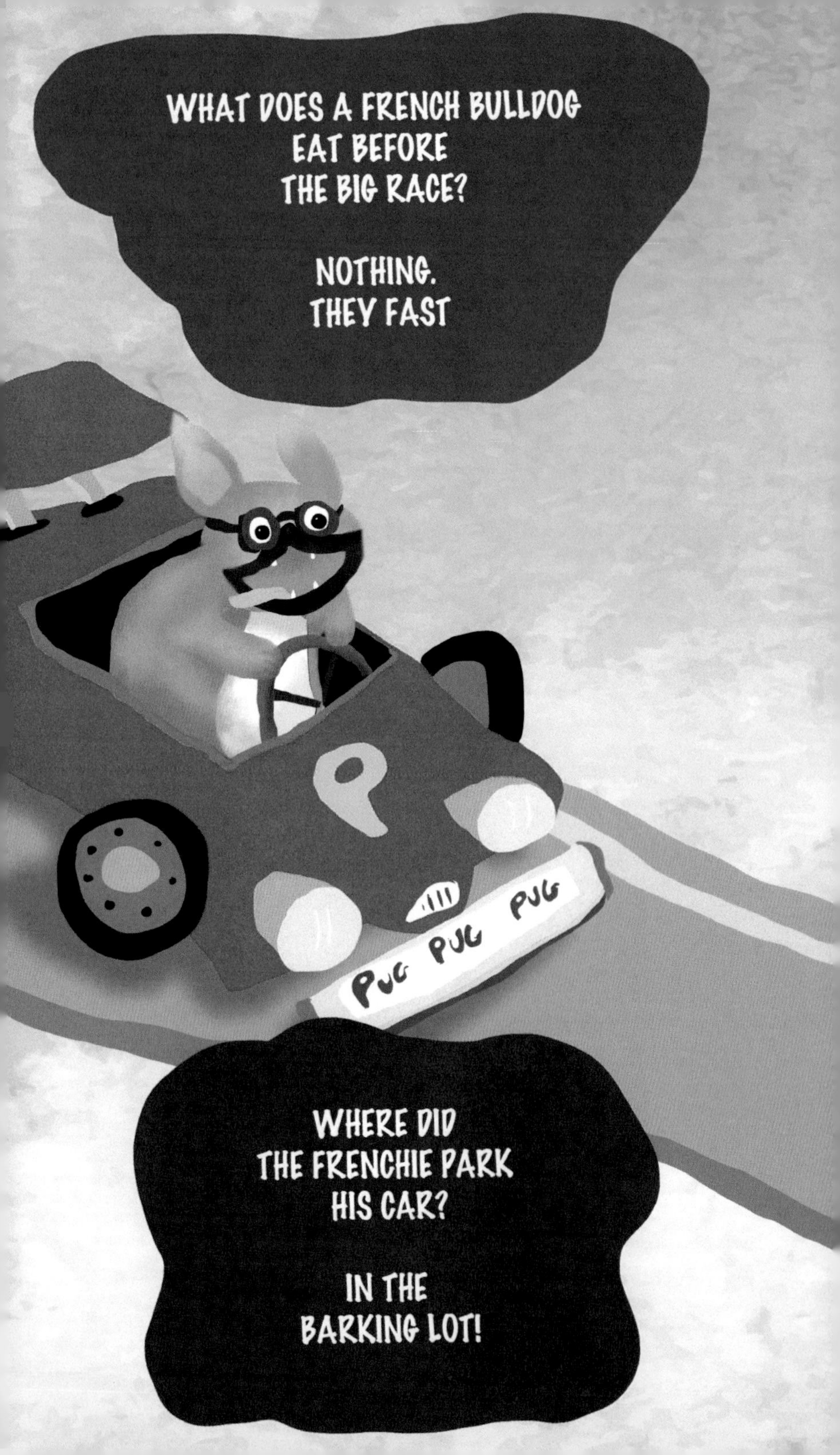
WHAT DOES A FRENCH BULLDOG EAT BEFORE THE BIG RACE?
NOTHING. THEY FAST
P
PUG PUG PUG
WHERE DID THE FRENCHIE PARK HIS CAR?
IN THE BARKING LOT!

WHY DID THE FRENCHIE
ROLL TOILET PAPER
DOWN THE HILL

SO IT COULD
GET TO THE BOTTOM

WHERE DID THE FRENCHIE
GO WHEN HIS
TAIL FELL OFF?

THE RETAIL STORE!

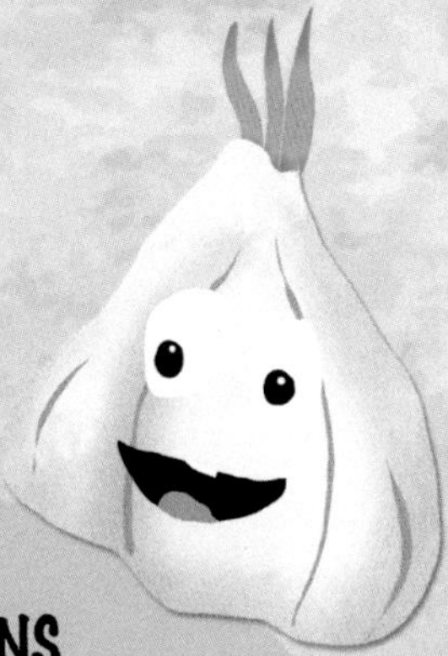

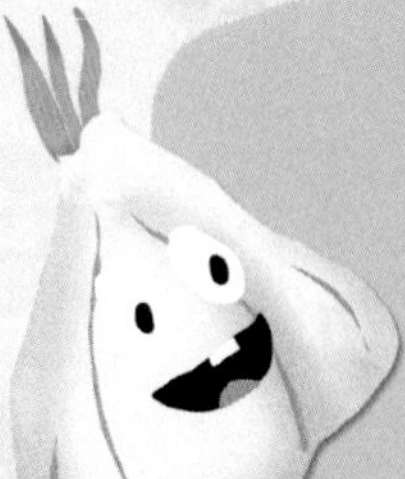

WHAT HAPPENS
WHEN THE FRENCH BULLDOG
ATE A CLOVE OF GARLIC?

HIS BARK
WAS WORSE THAN HIS BITE!

WHATS A FRENCH BULLDOGS
FAVORITE COMEDIAN?

GROWL-CHO MARX

ONE FRENCHIE
AND FOUR CATS
ARE IN A BOAT
THE FRENCHIE JUMPED OUT.
WHO IS LEFT IN THE BOAT?

NOBODY,
THEY WERE ALL
COPYCATS!

WHAT HAPPENED
WHEN THE CAT WON
THE FRENCH BULLDOG
BEAUTY CONTEST?

IT WAS A
CAT-HAS-TROPHY

WHAT DID
THE WINNER SAY?

CHECK
MEEEE-OUWT!

WHAT DO YOU GET
WHEN YOU CROSS A FRENCH BULLDOG
AND A HYENA?

I DON'T KNOW,
BUT IF IT LAUGHS, GIVE HIM A TREAT.

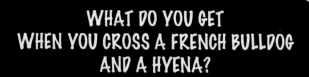

WHATS THE DIFFERENCE BETWEEN
A FRENCHIE AND A MARINE BIOLOGIST?

ONE WAGS A TALE,
THE OTHER
TAGS A WHALE!

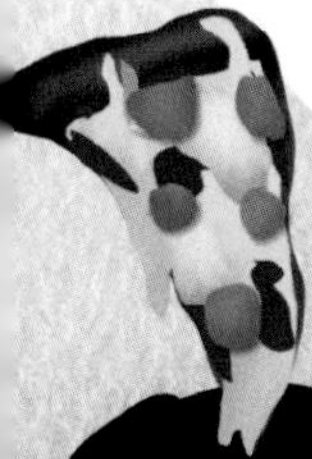

WHATS THE DIFFERENCE
BETWEEN MY FRENCH BULLDOG AND A PIZZA?

(DON'T KNOW)

IN THAT CASE, I'LL BE
ORDERING DINNER TONIGHT!

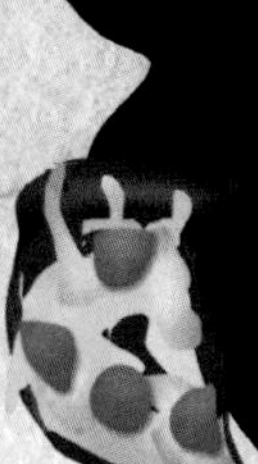

A FRENCHIE AT A
BASEBALL GAME KEPT WONDERING
WHY THE BALL WAS GETTING
BIGGER
AND BIGGER.

THEN IT HIT HIM!

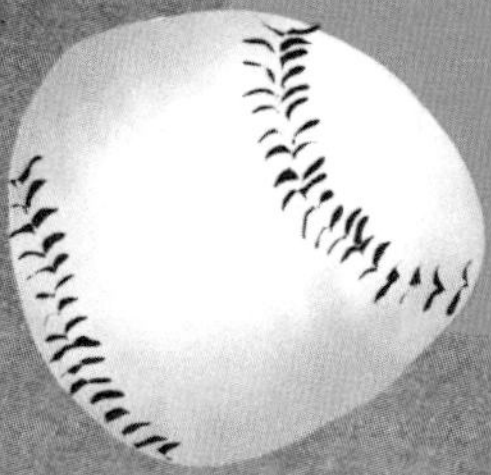

WHAT DO YOU MEAN,
MY FRENCHIE CHASED A GUY ON A BIKE?

MY FRENCHIE DOESN'T EVEN OWN A BIKE!

DID YOU HEAR
ABOUT THE FRENCH BULLDOG
WHO HAD NO NOSE?

I HEARD HE SMELLED
AWFUL!

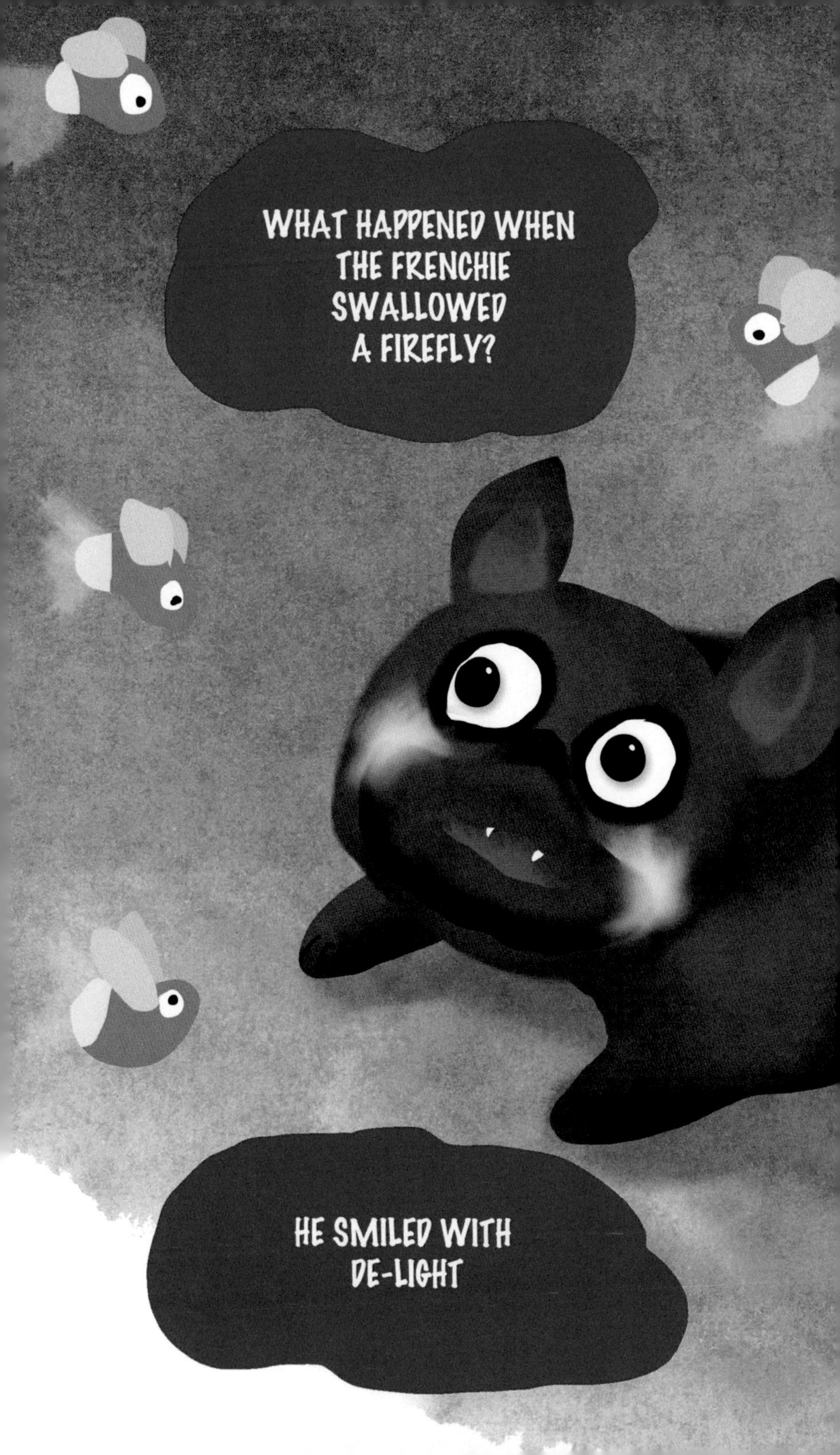
WHAT HAPPENED WHEN THE FRENCHIE SWALLOWED A FIREFLY?
HE SMILED WITH DE-LIGHT

WHAT DO YOU CALL A
FRENCHIE WITH A FEVER?

A HOT DOG!

WHAT ABOUT A COLD FRENCHIE?

A PUPSICLE

AND IF THAT FRENCHIE
GETS EVEN COLDER?

THAT'S A CHILI DOG!

WAIT! THAT COLD
FRENCHIE IS SITTING ON A RABBIT!

OH, THAT'S
A CHILI DOG ON A BUN!

WHAT DO MY FRENCH BULLDOG
AND MY PHONE HAVE IN COMMON?

THEY BOTH
HAVE COLLAR ID

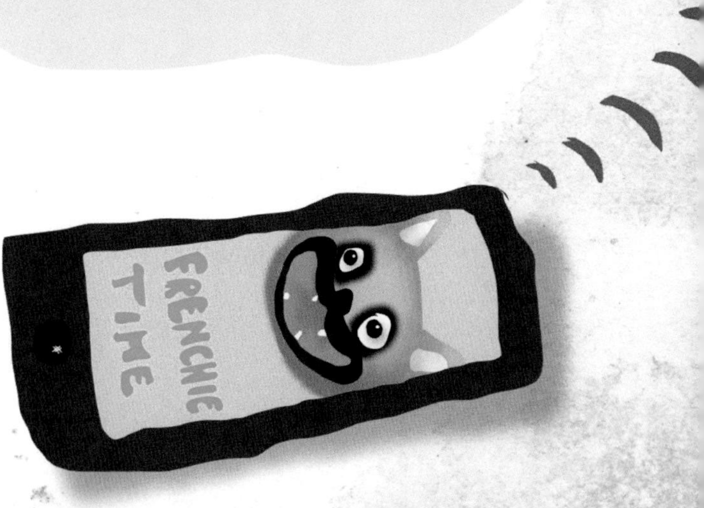
FRENCHIE
TIME

THE FRENCHIE TOLD HIS GIRLFRIEND
SHE DREW HER EYEBROWS
WAY TOO HIGH

SHE LOOKED VERY SURPRISED!

WHAT HAPPENED
WHEN THE FRENCH BULLDOG WENT
TO A FLEA CIRCUS?

HE STOLE THE SHOW

WHERE DO FRENCHIES HATE TO SHOP?

THE FLEA MARKET!

DID YOU HEAR
ABOUT THE SPECIAL AT
THE PET STORE?

BUY 1 DOG
GET ONE FLEA!

A FRENCHIE
WALKS INTO A BAR
ORDERS A DRINK
WHEN SUDDENLY HE HEARS
SOMEONE SHOUT "HEY CUTIE!"
THE FRENCHIE LOOKS AROUND BUT
NO ONE IS THERE
"HEY! NICE STUMPY TAIL!"
THE FRENCHIE LOOKS UP AGAIN
BUT NOBODY IS THERE.
"HEY! CUTE SHINY NOSE!"
THE FRENCHIE FRUSTRATED
CALLS OVER THE BARTENDER ASKING
"HEY, YOU TALKIN TO ME?"
THE BARTENDER REPLIES
"IT'S NOT ME!
IT'S THE COMPLMENTARY PEANUTS!"

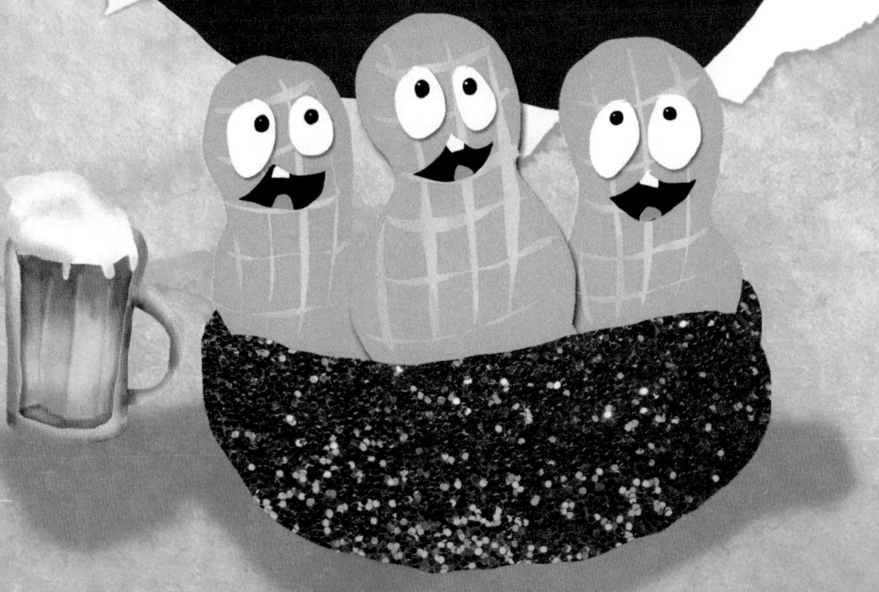

A
THREE LEGGED FRENCHIE
WALKS INTO A BAR
AND SAYS
"I'M LOOKING FOR THE MAN
WHO SHOT MY PAW"

WOULD YOU RATHER A
GIANT FRENCHIE CHASE YOU OR A LION?

I'D RATHER
HE CHASE THE LION!

WHAT DO YOU DO
WHEN YOU SEE YOUR FRENCHIE
EATING YOUR DICTIONARY?

TAKE THE WORDS
RIGHT OUT OF HIS MOUTH!

A FRENCHIE IS ON A BEACH
WATCHING A HIPPIE
DROWN IN THE WATER!

THE LIFEGUARD SAYS
"AREN'T YOU GONNA
DO SOMETHING?"

THE FRENCHIE REPLIES
"NO WAY,
HE'S TOO FAR OUT"

A FRENCHIE THINKS:
"WOW,
HUMANS BRING ME FOOD EVERY DAY,
THEY HAVE ME LIVE
IN A AWESOME HOUSE,
ITS NOT COLD, NO RAIN,
THEY TAKE CARE OF ME...
HUMANS MUST BE GODS..."

A CAT THINKS:
"WOW, HUMANS BRING ME FOOD EVERY DAY,
THEY HAVE ME LIVE IN A AWESOME HOUSE, I
TS NOT COLD, NO RAIN,
THEY TAKE CARE OF ME...
I MUST BE GOD!"

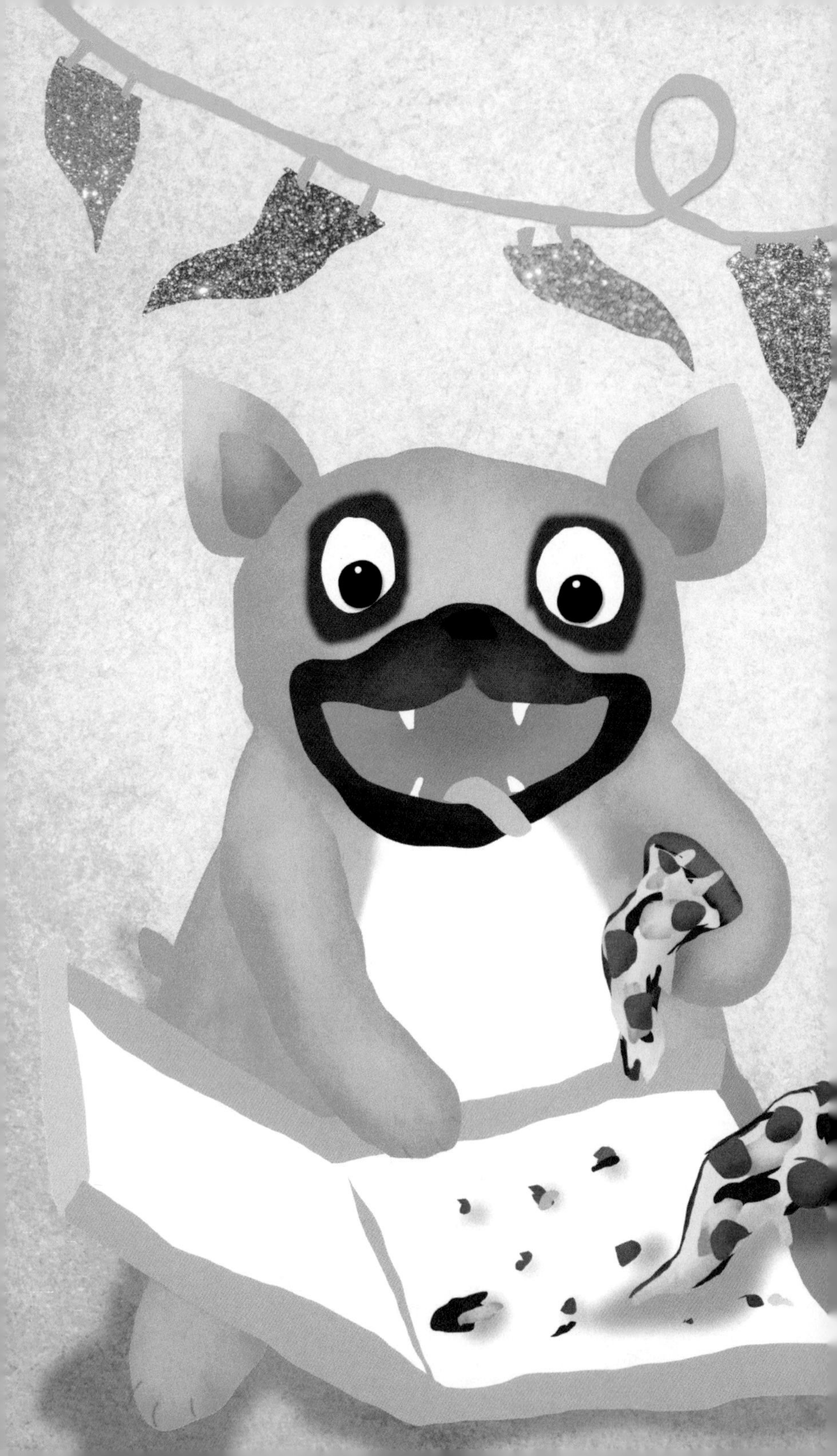

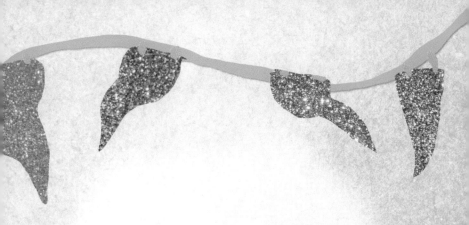

ABOUT THE AUTHOR

THE ULTIMATE FRENCH BULLDOG
JOKE BOOK WAS WRITTEN
BY FRANNIE D. FRENCHIE

FRANNIE IS A FUN LOVIN' FRENCHIE
FROM WISCONSIN
SHE LOVES TREATS,
SNUGGLES, PIZZA,
TELLING JOKES
AND WRITING BOOKS!